AUG – – 2019

PROPHECIES, PRAYERS & DECLARATIONS

BREAKTHROUGH

SHAWN BOLZ

Published by ICreate Productions,
PO Box 50219, Studio City, CA 91614
www.bolzministries.com

To contact the author about speaking at your conference or church,
please go to www.bolzministries.com

Edited by Kyle Duncan

ISBN: 978-1-949709-29-2

eBook ISBN: 978-1-949709-35-3

Printed in the United States of America

TABLE OF CONTENTS

How to Use This Book -- vii

Introduction -- xv

Relationships --- 1

Relational Hardships --- 11

Influence/Favor--- 23

Healing --31

Mental and Emotional Health --------------------------------- 43

Grief and Loss--- 53

Transition --- 65

Restoration and Redemption --------------------------------- 73

Finances--- 83

Business and Career--91

Church and Ministry --103

Spiritual Warfare---113

To Become a Breaker in Every Area-------------------------- 125

HOW TO USE THIS BOOK

WHY POWER OF DECLARATION, PROPHECIES, AND PRAYER?

Throughout human history we have seen the power of prayer, the impact of the prophetic, and the symbolism of declarations having huge impact to shape societies, set culture, provide heritage, and bring vision for the future. I wrote this book so you would have a very specific tool to help you use words to define your own history and future with God. I love the power of prayer, prophecy, and declaration, and these have been weapons in my own life to create the context of faith and intimacy I am now living in. I see these three verbal tools as some of the most important definers of our relationships, vision, and calling in life.

Prayer helps us to commune with God's nature and heart. We get to converse with God with listening ears. We get to share our pain, victory, struggles, and inner life with God. Through prayer, we allow the Holy Spirit to share space in God's heart with us, and we experience being one with Him each time.

Prophecies are God's will, accompanied by His love declared over us. They give us an opportunity to align our faith in connection to what we believe about ourselves. They help our humanity catch up to His spirit. Prophecies create sight for the gap between what is not yet happening and what God desires to do in our lives, and they help us to engage a process of relationship with God through faith to close that gap. Prophecies change our opportunities, ignite our potential, and cause us to have a chance to live beyond the fruit we can attain by our own efforts.

Declarations are when we speak out loud *on purpose for purpose.* These are our statements of faith aligning us to God's will and directives for our lives and the world around us.

Life is in the power of the tongue: "Death and life are in the power of the tongue, and those who love it will eat its fruit" (Proverbs 18:21). As Christians and emotionally intelligent humans, we see that the tongue is our most powerful tool or weapon. It has the power to release life wherever we go. People who understand this will speak intentionally and will eat the abundant fruit their past words (declarations) have produced. We will speak to others and to ourselves because we realize silence is indifference and passivity is a thief. Declarations help us to be intentional and therefore aware of when God does move, because we are declaring and then looking for the fulfillment of very specific statements.

When you combine prayers, declarations, and prophecies as I have in this book, you are even more intentional about the power of words. In the book of Joel, Joel lays out a prophetic picture of people realizing the time and season they were in and said they beat their plowshares into swords and their pruning hooks into spears. That is what I hope to accomplish here: that the words you have used to cultivate faith in your identity, calling, and destiny would now become weapons as you speak them out over yourself and everyone you are involved with.

Words are tools and weapons that propel us forward to lay hold of all that Jesus won for us: "Your very words will be used as evidence against you, and your words will declare you either innocent or guilty" (Matthew 12:37). This verse is obviously not talking about being saved through godly speaking, but it does imply our declarations will either restrict or bless our lives. Using our words deliberately will propel us into the abundant life Jesus promised us. Instead of setting up boundaries of limitation and restriction in our experience (aka being condemned, according to Matthew 12:37), we will be able to engage and live out our lives through Christ we make declarations about.

Prayers, declarations, and prophecies are instrumental for us to enter our promised land: "Always remember what is written in that book of law. Speak about that book and study it day and night. Then you can be sure to obey what is written there. If you do this, you will be wise and successful in everything you do" (Joshua 1:8).

God spoke to Joshua and told him to implement nonstop speaking of truth as he made final preparations to possess what God had already given through promise. Joshua is our example to use prayers, declarations, and even the prophetic words we have as a means to possessing the promises of God.

Using prayers, prophecies, and declarations to activate our faith for things that don't yet exist in our lives is one of our greatest ways to be like our model, Jesus: "For in God's presence he believed that God can raise the dead and call into being things that don't even exist yet" (Romans 4:17).

As a Christian you won't just be aware of injustice or brokenness; you will be aware of the fact that through Jesus, anything can be redeemed or restored. You start to understand the Spirit of God, who is focused on bringing life to dead places, people, nations, and gifts, and who calls for someone to say it is alive when it still looks dead.

You also get to see into His heart and original plan or intention in everything He created. Through this you will begin to have the opportunity to speak to situations, people, and purposes, calling forth what doesn't "even exist yet."

We see lots of scriptural examples of people using prophetic words, prayers, and declarations to be an articulate tool in their relationship to their faith and connection to God, themselves, and the world.

Through this book I invite you on a journey to use words to speak into the very fabric of your life, the spiritual realm, and the world around you. These words are all tools for you to align your faith and create your inner life as one full of courage and hope. You will find yourself using your own language at times or tailoring the words I have written for you, and that is exactly what you should do! Make it apply deeply and closely to you and your situation.

Words create space and need space to be created, so I encourage you to find alone time or time with a partner and allow these words to come out of your mouth—out loud! If you don't feel faith when you are saying a declaration, say it many times and allow the words to become more familiar to your heart. If you can't own the goodness of one of the prophetic words, then say it repeatedly with your name in it so it's yours. With prayers, make sure you aren't just religiously repeating what is on paper but are actually picturing yourself in the prayer. These are your tools, your words, and you have to own them and make them work for you. Eventually, as you read this, you will even beat these words into weapons and you will see results.

Practically, the book is laid out over several subjects, using the theme of breakthrough to empower your faith. None of them are quite the same because I didn't want to give you a formula; I wanted to help you develop language and some models for how you will use the powerful tools of prophecy, prayer, and declaration. The way we declare in one theme might seem totally different to the next. Sometimes the prophecies are first person; sometimes they are the stated intention of God as I have received it for you.

Maybe you need the specific subject heading to lead you right now, or maybe you want to visit each of them in a row to prophesy, declare, and pray into your life. Maybe some of them won't feel authentic to the way you express yourself or receive; or maybe some just won't apply directly to you. Don't get hung up on the individual part; just keep moving forward and find what you can own and what can help you to bring about a greater breakthrough in your life.

I pray you will find yourself using and reusing this book, as well as hearing God for yourself. I encourage you to underline specific phrases in each section you are coming into agreement with. Say the prayers until they are your prayers; own the prophecies, because they are for you. Make declarations with your family and say them until they are part of your DNA. Most of all, let this be your book as though you manufactured each part yourself.

"A new song for a new day rises up in me every time I think about how he breaks through for me! Ecstatic praise pours out of my mouth until everyone hears how God has set me free. Many will see his miracles; they'll stand in awe of God and fall in love with him!"

Psalm 40:3 TPT

INTRODUCTION

WHERE DOES THE THEME OF BREAKTHROUGH COME FROM?

The theme of breakthrough appears everywhere in our world—in science when someone finds a breakthrough technology, in the military when there is a movement or advance past the enemy's line, in entertainment when a project does something that has never been done before or someone has a breakout role, in society when there is a sudden shift or forward movement in an issue that was previously oppressed or misunderstood. We see the theme of having a breakthrough in all areas of life and in the world.

I love how we see breakthrough appear in the Bible because it is one of the definers of God. It shows His name, character, and desire to break us out of oppression or bring us breakthrough into His promises. In some modern Christian circles, this has become another inspirational buzzword, and it is at times. But when the Bible uses the terms about breakthrough, the words are never hypothetical or just inspirational; they are absolute about the nature of God.

For example, my favorite place it appears is when David names a place with a name he identifies as God. It is one of the biggest slaps in the face to his rivals, the Philistines, because David hijacks their own god's name and puts our God above him. In

2 Samuel 5:20, we read, "So David went to Baal-perazim and defeated the Philistines there. 'The Lord did it!' David exclaimed. 'He burst through my enemies like a raging flood!' So he named that place Baal-perazim (which means 'the Lord who breaks or bursts through')" (NLT).

David is proclaiming this by using the example of how waters during floods break through or burst out, making new streams. The water can't be confined. When water breaks out of its banks, awesome, visible power is displayed as the water pushes past everything in its way. David describes the power of God in a similar way because when God is upon a situation, His breakthrough, there is nothing that can stop it.

Before this breakthrough happened for David and Israel, the scene in the Scripture is called Valley of Rephaim, meaning "house of the giant." But here is what is awesome: After the breakthrough, it is called *Ba'al Perazim*, meaning "Possessor of Breaches, Lord of the Breakthrough."

One of the most awesome parts of this theme of David naming it this was that he used the name of Ba'al, a god of the Philistines, to define it. He did this as a reminder that at this place, the enemy thought he was the strongest. So David called it *Baal Perazim*, declaring that God broke through the stronghold of the enemy! He named his God above all the little giants of Baal. This still happens for us today: God breaks through in awesome ways that belittle our enemies and cause the oppression against us to look small in comparison to His strength.

Spiritual breakthrough isn't just about breaking off something; it is also about advancing in unprecedented ways. Both of these have always been themes in the Bible and in history. We tell the stories of how God broke through and transformed the world, shifted countries, and engaged culture through believers like you and me, who dared to believe with radical faith.

True and lasting breakthrough starts in your identity and heart, the very core of who you are and what you believe. You have to know God as the One who wants your breakthrough from hardship and breakthrough into promise more than you do. It is part of His revealed biblical role as a Father to you to bring breakthrough to you; and the more you get to know Him, the more you expect that the process of building relationship with Him brings about great breakthroughs in your family, opportunities, and goals—but it all comes from the core process of building connection with Him.

As I show here, breakthrough isn't just a catchphrase but one of God's very names in the Bible. God wants to reveal Himself as your Lord who breaks through, just like Micah prophesied to the Israelites. Micah 2:13 says, "One who breaks open the way will go up before them; they will break through the gate and go out. Their king will pass through before them, the Lord at their head."

In verse 13, "breaker" appears to be the title for an individual who will rescue the Israelites—the breaker: the one who goes ahead, breaks down obstacles, and leads the way! In Hebrew it is the phrase *ha poretz*. This is the only time in the Bible that the phrase *ha poretz* appears to be the title of an individual. It is speaking about the Messiah for the Israelites and is still one of the ways He wants us to relate to Him today.

Knowing God as the one who goes ahead of you for your breakthrough, leading you, is one of the most comforting ways to know God. It also will give you the courage to blaze trails in areas of life not many people would risk or dare to go in—because they don't have a relationship through their faith, like you do, to trust they will arrive at a destination.

When we begin to pray into our own lives and apply the Bible to our circumstances, we start to see the effects of our God, our breaker, not just helping us but also creating His original plan in our lives and not letting anything interfere with it.

Making declarations, prayers, and prophetic statements or words about breakthrough has been done throughout history, but no one did this better than King David.

Psalm 18 is a perfect picture of David pouring his heart out to God. He shares about how God protected him, how God broke through for him where he was oppressed, and how God delivered him into his promise. He also declares the nature of God and defines breakthrough, the promise of God, and how that promise was fulfilled. Read it in The Passion Translation and it can help you see what I am attempting to do in a modern way through this book to give you tools to partner your inner cry and faith.

We see David pouring out his heart in prayer, declaring who God is, sharing the prophetic belief system that carried him through the hardships, and sharing the breakthrough into his appointment as king. It's such a radical picture of viewing the God who breaks through. And as you read through these prayers, you will find yourself writing your own story after using this tool for your life.

"In order to be able to make and keep commitments... to enduring, intimate relationships... you need to be a certain kind of person. You need to be a powerful person. Powerful people take responsibility for their lives and choices. Powerful people choose who they want to be with, what they are going to pursue in life, and how they are going to go after it."

–Danny Silk

RELATIONSHIPS

FAMILY, SPOUSE, KIDS,
FRIENDS, AND COMMUNITY

*"As for me and my house,
we will serve the Lord."*

Joshua 24:15

*"God sets the lonely in families, he leads out
the prisoners with singing; but the rebellious
live in a sun-scorched land."*

Psalm 68:6

Here are your keys for breakthrough in your relationships. God's breakthrough works best on this side of eternity for the goal or purpose of relationship.

BREAKTHROUGH PROPHECY

Part of experiencing My breakthrough for you is allowing Me to make your family, friends, and community one of your primary promised-land experiences. I have made you for relationships and I will surround you with them. I am creating your inner and outer circle with you and for you as the expression of My heart to reveal the deepest part of My love to you and through you to them. You are a powerful developer of family, friends, and community through Me. I have created within you everything you need to express My love to your spouse, your children, your parents, your siblings, your friends, and your community. I have given you the ability to produce healthy and powerful relationships. Ask for My love and I will give you the emotional intelligence to express it in epic ways.

Through your relationships I am going to bring about the most connectedness you could ever feel. I am going to bring the right attachment to you and each of your relationships and it will sustain you through the hard times; but it will also be one of the greatest celebratory devices you could possibly experience.

I am going to bring an incubator of purpose through your closest relationships. You will not feel alone or isolated. My desire for you is to have relationships that will bring out My colors and My image from your life. I am going to use your social circle to bring you courage to take giant leaps of faith.

I have given you the ability to have breakthrough in your relational situations through My will and desire for you in situations that would normally break down families or relationships. When you are wounded or hurt by something your relational circle does or says, lean into Me and I will bring My breakthrough into your very being. I will cause the wounds to build a deeper connection with Me and to them, even when things get damaged or feel unreconcilable. I will restore your heart and I can restore your relationship to them, even if it looks broken. I will give you forgiveness and reconnect you.

You are not alone; your relationships are some of the greatest treasures I will use to develop My nature in you—and you can trust My nature. I sent My Son, Jesus, so He could reconcile you to My original plan: connection to Me and connection to other people. Your relationships are a powerful tool that can be the greatest display of what eternal life looks like because of your love for one another. Your love for others will help people want to know Me, to know My Son. People will know this is what they were made for as well. People will see your marriage, your fathering or mothering, your extended family, your close friendships, and watch you work through the same struggles but with the help of My spirit, who will lead you into deeper love instead of drifting apart.

People will see how you love even when someone needs correction. You will not punish but will bring about conviction and discipline that will cause them to trust you and bond to you even more. Your family will display My intention of love to your community. It is meant to be a picture of My breakthrough to the world. People will be filled with so much hope through watching you love well relationally.

I will cause you to be such a family person. Your family is also meant to be everlasting; the way you are building with them now will have a reflection in eternity. Love well, love like Me, and I will pour My ever-refilling love back into you.

PRAYER

God, I ask You to empower me by implementing Your original plan over my family and relational structure. Bring the breakthrough needed to bring Your purpose over us into being through Your divine love. Give me the right alignment of connection with each friend and family member I have. Help me to prioritize sharing my life with them with my time, energy, resources, emotions, and spirit. Show me how to pray for them and enlarge my capacity to understand them.

Even through hardship in certain relationships, I pray, Holy Spirit, that You would keep me thinking and believing with the Father's perspective. Gift me with breakthrough faith for each circumstance and for each person You have called me to love. Help me not to live out of just my experience with each person but out of Yours. You know each of them so intimately. You know what is in their hearts. You know their motives, their desires, their strengths, and their destinies. Help me to know them like You do. Help me connect to them in ways that demonstrate how much I treasure them. Help me to not just treat them according to how I see them but according to how You do.

When my relational circle struggles through grief, hardship, or loss, I pray I would have faith in Your breakthrough power to bring about Your plan—one so different to mine were I left to my own human process. Help us to come together and strengthen each other. Keep us all from doing life alone or in isolation. Help us to rely on each other as we rely on You and Your strength.

I pray I would be a source of strength, love, and identity for each person in my life, sharing not only my time with them but also my very life. Form our interdependence by keeping us from any codependence or unhealthy patterns. Help us to have unity in our homes and peace in our hearts. Give us grace for mistakes.

Even as You are love, let us be love to one another: patient, kind, slow to anger, generous. I pray You would help me to make choices toward love even when I feel hurt or frustrated.

I pray for each person in my relational circle to have the power to break through into Your John 10:10 desire for them to truly thrive. I ask that You would bring us into Your thriving plan and break off any of the plans of the enemy—who comes to steal, kill, and destroy.

God of the breakthrough, bring breakthrough to my relationships!

DECLARATION

I declare that the God of breakthrough is making me a powerful builder of family, relationships, and community. I am empowered to create an amazing family through marriage, childbirth, and adoption; through creating epic friendships; and through being a leader to my extended family and a real member who blesses my community.

I believe everyone in my family and friendship network will have an opportunity to know and fully love God because of our connection. I declare that my whole household will be saved, walking in their full connection with God in complete destiny.

My family, household, and relationships will be blessed! We will be blessed in our extended families, careers, spiritual gifts, talents, and opportunities. In everything we do and everywhere we go, the God of breakthrough will help us succeed. He surrounds us with favor like a shield, and no weapon formed against us can prosper. What the Lord has blessed, no one can curse.

The God of breakthrough is bringing my family into their promised land, both individually and corporately. He will author and finish His will for us in our lifetimes, and nothing will be cut short.

God will break through any places we get stuck in relationally or financially, in our health, or in any other area that would bring about pain, destruction, or brokenness. God will cut off any plans of the enemy to steal from us, kill us, or destroy our connections. He will bring us into the life He planned for us, a life that is abundant and full through our Savior, Jesus Christ.

"Love isn't when there are
no fights in the relationship.
Love is when once the fight ends,
love is still there."

—Unknown

RELATIONAL HARDSHIPS

BETRAYAL, ACCUSATION,
SLANDER, CONFLICT

"And we know that all things work together
for good to those who love God, to those who
are the called according
to His purpose."

Romans 8:28

"Even when bad things happen to the good
and godly ones, the Lord will save them and
not let them be defeated by
what they face."

Psalm 34:19 TPT

"Let the sunrise of your love end our dark
night. Break through our clouded dawn
again! Only you can satisfy our hearts,
filling us with songs of joy to the
end of our days."

Psalm 90:14 TPT

*"Don't be pulled in different directions
or worried about a thing. Be saturated
in prayer throughout each day, offering
your faith-filled requests before God with
overflowing gratitude. Tell him every detail
of your life, then God's wonderful peace
that transcends human understanding,
will make the answers known to you
through Jesus Christ. So keep your thoughts
continually fixed on all that is authentic and
real, honorable and admirable, beautiful
and respectful, pure and holy, merciful and
kind. And fasten your thoughts on every
glorious work of God, praising him always.
Follow the example of all that we have
imparted to you and the God of peace will
be with you in all things."*

Philippians 4:6–9

Here are your keys for breakthrough in relational hardships. The world is filled with conflict but Jesus died so we could navigate with an operational system of love.

BREAKTHROUGH PROPHECY

The Breaker of heaven will break through for you in a very real way. God understands the work of betrayal, slander, and conflict because of facing off against both angels and men who have worked against Him. Jesus Himself was surrounded by it on Earth. He never turns His eyes from seeing or hearing injustice on Earth. He does have a plan to restore everything you feel is lost, wounded, or broken, and Jesus paid the ultimate price to redeem and restore your heart no matter how much hurt you have faced.

God wants to develop in you strength reserves you didn't know you could have—they come from Him living inside you. He is giving you the ability to have breakthrough from the trauma of relational pain.

He is going to give you insight at times into why the person who hurt you did what they did and this will cause deep compassion in your heart and help you to not take on the offense of the pain.

The God whose name is Breakthrough is going to give you power to not become bitter, to not get stuck, to not have cyclical thoughts of pain because of this wounding. He is not going to let the wound get infected if you lean into Him. He desires to heal you in such a way that actually uses what the enemy intended for evil to be used to strengthen you.

He will teach you so much through this so that your pain has meaning and can set others free. He will not let a demonic spin be on top of the pain to bring added confusion, pain, or suffering. He will deliver you from being haunted in the night hours by fear, anxiety, threat, stress, or the replaying of negative words toward you.

Fear is not your destiny or identity. Betrayal is not your story. Slander is not your finish line. Your forgiveness toward those who were the instigators of this attack will be the Holy Spirit's doorway to bring about His justice for you. God will have full reign to destroy the work of the enemy and to write His narrative of goodness. Those who fight against you and dishonor you actually dishonor God within you and they will reap what they sow, but you will leave these things behind and fly like you had the wings of an eagle, run without weariness, and walk through relationships without getting tired.

He will show you how to release relationships that have become toxic where the person is making a choice against you. He will also show you when to hold onto a hope against all odds for relationships He wants to radically restore.

PRAYER

God, I forgive [name the person], who did this to me. I release them and the responsibility they have to You. I trust You to be the God who breaks through all the damage that was done and who heals everything. I pray You would take away haunting thoughts, emotions, and hurt. I also pray You would give me a strategy and would counsel me on how to hold my heart with this person. Give me Your resolve that is based on Your desire and Your love, not just on mine.

Work deep inside me to keep my faith and hope alive. I pray that my love for You and for others would grow and not be wounded. Help me to learn from this experience so I can grow in my ability to love and be loved. Let my heart not shut down.

Help me to express my feelings and disappointments no matter how much vulnerability it takes. Help me to know who to confide in, and help me to not be afraid to process what is happening inside me so I can get insight about what You are doing as well. Help me to not talk about any persons in a way that would harm their reputation or change anyone's attitude toward them. Let me honor them even if I wasn't honored.

Give me the courage to use a healthy conflict model that is directed toward resolution. Help me to not be a conflict avoider. God, give my heart the ability to fight for love and health and the relational strength to confront when I need to confront, with the right goal of giving them the opportunity to change. Give me Your loving words and clarity of thought when I am processing confrontation and pain.

I know You won't just help but will also make my outcome better than if the hurtful moment(s) hadn't happened in the first place.

DECLARATION

I declare breakthrough over this relationship! I know God causes everything to work together for my good, no matter what the circumstance against me. I will trust in faith that He will bring relational alignment to me in accordance with His purpose.

I declare that the Breaker will break off any of the effects of sin's harm toward me. I declare and decree that because God is for me, no one can stand against me!

Even when someone slanders me, betrays me, rejects me, causes me harm, or persecutes me, God is a shield around me, keeping me from everlasting pain.

I declare that no one is able to bring an unfitting charge against me as one of God's chosen people, for God is the One who causes me to be considered righteous! I declare that nothing is able to separate us from the love of the Lord: not trouble, hardship, persecution, hunger, poverty, danger or war.

In all things I am more than a conqueror, through the One who loves us!

I also declare that lies or misunderstandings will fall off any mutual relationships from the person who instigated these against me. I will not lose other relationships that God gave me because of this person's choice. No matter what they say, God will protect what He has built in my life.

I am convinced that neither death nor life, neither angels nor other heavenly rulers, neither what exists nor what is coming, neither powers above nor powers below, nor any other created thing is able to separate me from the love of God that comes to me through Christ Jesus.

Therefore, I will not stay or be discouraged by troubles but will trust the Holy Spirit to use it all for God's glory.

I receive the Holy Spirit's empowerment within me to bring me new inner strength and to take the sting of death out of memories, relationships, interactions, and attitudes of others.

Although love has been violated against me, I choose to be rooted and founded in God's love, knowing this love will bring a cleansing and unifying to everyone who is safe for me to be in true relationship with.

I open my heart to be vulnerable to all the healthy love God has for me, and I choose to risk in relationship even though I was hurt. I allow God to be the keeper of my heart and to give me fresh strength and grace to be made whole and to start fresh in my relational capacity.

I declare that I am worth being in relationship with and I will only spend my relational value where God shows me and where it is wise.

"Influence is when you are not the one talking and yet your words fill the room; when you are absent and yet your presence is felt everywhere."

—TemitOpe Ibrahim

INFLUENCE/FAVOR

"You are the salt of the earth, but if salt has lost its taste, how shall its saltiness be restored? It is no longer good for anything except to be thrown out and trampled under people's feet. You are the light of the world. A city set on a hill cannot be hidden. Nor do people light a lamp and put it under a basket, but on a stand, and it gives light to all in the house. In the same way, let your light shine before others, so that they may see your good works and give glory to your Father who is in heaven."

Matthew 5:13–16 ESV

"O God, make the king a godly judge like you and give the king's son the gift of justice too. Help him to give true justice to your people, honorably and equally to all. Then the mountains of influence will be fruitful, and from your righteousness prosperity and peace will flow to all the people."

Psalm 72:1–3

Two of the main keys to heaven's breakthrough are the influence and favor God gives us through working within and outside of us. Christians experience uncommon influence so they can have uncommonly fruitful lives the world isn't worthy of—just like Jesus!

BREAKTHROUGH PROPHECY

I have made you to be an influencer in your family, relationships, city, region, industry, and culture. Just as Daniel, Joseph, and Esther in the Bible were raised up to places of influence, so too I have created you to shine like a lamp and I want to put you on the highest lamp stand in the highest place so My light in you can illuminate the world with love. I have created you to have favor that will display My love toward the world.

Your breakthrough is everyone else's breakthrough around you because when you get influence it will be a highway between heaven and Earth of resource, counsel, strategy, and connection. I am sending you on unique assignments and you will wonder how you got there because you are not always going to be skilled enough or you will not always be doing what you are educated for. Sometimes it will be to people you can't relate to in the natural; other times it will be someone older or younger than you to whom you don't have the expertise to relate. When I send you to these people, they will know I sent you because the whole earth is waiting to see if I love and care about what they do and you will show up and be My face. You will give them hope, courage, wisdom, and strength to see what is within them.

As you influence people with My heart, you will grow in influence and ability to steer situations. The world throws money at solving problems, the world throws manipulation at solving relational challenges, but I am going to use creativity through you to help bring about different solutions. As I bring wisdom upon your life, you will bring a different option, a different way of thinking that is beyond what people can manufacture through their own skills, talents, and abilities. You will prove that I am a God who loves and that I love them.

When I give you influence, it is so that people will know that I love them. The Queen of Sheba told Solomon, "Surely your God loves His people because He raised up a man like you to lead them." People of influence will watch how you steward your influence at your workplace, in your industry, in your family, in your relationships, and they will say, "Surely God loves you and your family because He has raised you up this way."

PRAYER

God, make me a person of influence. Let my life carry as much light as I can contain. Put me in the highest place of influence I can carry in this life so I can bring the most light. I wasn't made to be hidden under a bowl; I was made to shine brightly from the greatest position You dreamed of for me. I pray that You would deliver me from the desire to be small or hidden from fear of pride or influence. Let me not have false humility, which the wrong kind of religion brings, but let me have joy in shining Your reputation through me. Help me to not limit myself because of what I don't have in skill, talent, education, or charisma, and help me to be limited by Your spirit within me, which has no limitations!

Let influence be part of my life whether I am known by many or by few. Let my life influence others in times when it feels like I'm in prison and in times of reigning, like Joseph's. Let my significance not come from who I get to be but from who You are in me. I pray that I would be able to see that being a temple of Your spirit means I have to honor Your influence through me and not try to back away from it or take credit for it.

I pray that You would help me to see my life as a container of grace for others. Even as Your Holy Spirit lives in me, I ask You, Holy Spirit to be a counselor, comforter, and friend through me to the world around me. Give me all the influence my life can hold so I can see You get Your great reward, Jesus. Amen.

*"May undeserved favor and endless peace
be yours continually from our Father God
and from our Lord Jesus,
the Anointed One!"*

2 Corinthians 1:2

*"And Jesus grew in wisdom and stature, and
in favor with God and man."*

Luke 2:52

*"The Lord bless you, and keep you; the Lord
make his face shine on you and be gracious
to you; the Lord turn his face toward you
and give you peace."*

Numbers 6:24–26

DECLARATION

I set my faith to believe You want me to be a person of influence. You have designed me to carry Your strength, perspective, and wisdom so I can benefit the world around me. You have given me influence so I can prove that You love Your people. You have made me a Solomon so that people like the Queen of Sheba will know of Your great love.

I declare that You are worthy to use my life in every way You dreamed of to influence the world around me. I am not limited to my expertise or lack thereof. You are not limited by my abilities or lack of abilities. You are going to use me in ways that don't make sense to the world around me and sometimes through faith don't even make sense to me until I obey and see Your purpose unfold.

I declare that I will obey You and love people with the healthy agenda of love instead of the religious agenda of making them like me. I know that as I love well, people will seek me out for advice, counsel, wisdom, strategy, hope, and love, and they will know You are living in me. I commit to giving them an opportunity to know You the way I know You. Amen.

"*Let it be a settled fact: It is God's will to heal you. You have a right to healing as well as forgiveness when you believe. God said: I am the Lord who heals you (Ex 15:26). If God said this, and God cannot lie, He meant it. What God says is true. So, healing is yours. Healing is part of the gospel and is to be preached throughout the world to every creature to the need of the world.*"

–T. L. Osborn,
Healing the Sick: A Divine Healing Classic for Everyone

"*Those who are healthy become instruments of healing.*"

–Anonymous

HEALING

*"Dear friend, I pray that you may enjoy
good health and that all may go well with
you, even as your soul is getting along well."*

3 John 1:2

*"But he was pierced for our rebellion,
crushed for our sins. He was beaten so we
could be whole. He was whipped so
we could be healed."*

Isaiah 53:5

*"Let all that I am praise the Lord; may I
never forget the good things He does for me.
He forgives all my sins and heals
all my diseases."*

Psalm 103:2–3 NLT

You have the keys of breakthrough for your health. God has designed your body from the beginning of time to serve His will in your life and He never imagined you sick, diseased, or injured. He wants to close the gap between health issues and the reality of His provision of health for you. He wants to show you how to live in health and also to receive healing when you need it.

BREAKTHROUGH PROPHECY

I want to bring breakthrough to your health! When I dreamed of you and created you, there were no flaws, defects, or issues with your body that were part of My creative plan. I want to give you insight on what to do to sow into your everyday health. When you are sick or injured or have a disease, I want to restore it to exactly how I intended your body to work at this stage in your life. I created you to be able to have full strength and energy for everything I put inside of you to accomplish, for every person I have given you to love, for every dream I have given you to live out. You need your full health for the full life I have called you to live.

I am placing resources of exercise, supplements, healthy foods, the power of water, and healthy patterns all around you. Let Me gently lead you each day to participate with My health plan for your life. Allow yourself to be nudged by My spirit over food, water, exercise, and self-care. You will accumulate each day as you obey simple steps that aren't a formula, diet, or strenuous way of living. My yoke is easy and My burden is light even for health. The way you live will be a breakthrough from generational conditions and unhealthy patterns in family traditions, and your friends and family will take notice and see Me at work within you through My design of your body, My temple. Love your body; I made it for you. And don't let the areas you are disappointed in cause self-hate or self-harm, because I love you. I look at you as My grand creation, My masterpiece. When you see yourself through My eyes, you will celebrate your body. You won't look at what is not; you will see what is and you will see how beautifully and wonderfully you are made. Let Me show you the *you* in your body I created.

I know that in this world there are so many health issues; they didn't come from Me or My will. The only thing I ask is that you remain open in faith and believe this isn't what I intended for you and that you can be healed. Live in your heart as though this isn't My story for you. Don't settle for it to be your personal truth when I have so much more for you. Hope against hope; dare to invite Me to have a different report than doctors; don't let your heart close when the report is different from Mine. Keep your spiritual curiosity open for what I can do for you even if you haven't seen Me move this way before. I have given you some pictures and stories I made sure you heard through the Bible and in real life so you would have a history of hearing what I could do for others, because I want to do something huge for you.

I love you, and part of the way a natural father would love his afflicted child is to use everything within his means to get that child help. I sent My Son and He was broken and bruised for you. I didn't just pay the price by sending Him; we overpaid it so you could have full access to My original intention over your body, even now before your everlasting life in heaven.

I am bringing you breakthrough, and even your story of how you saw My spirit overcome your suffering will help others know how much I love you and them. I will give you insight about My nature even when you don't understand the circumstances. I won't allow your suffering to be prolonged when you call out to Me. I am going to walk with you every step of your healing journey.

Don't let fear in. Don't let weariness change your faith story that is unraveling. Keep to the simplicity of love and of healing. Don't let others try to make you earn your healing through a religious spirit that tries to get you to pray all kinds of prayers, working hard at trying to get healed. Rest in Me and receive My love. When healthy people pray for you, let it build My compassion and care toward you. Expect your miracle like it is going to come each day. Don't get discouraged if it doesn't come instantly, but allow your heart to be childlike—in faith as if it could.

I will not let any days be wasted. I will multiply your time, energy, and resources—everything the enemy is trying to steal. I will give you and your loved ones strength, and I will empower you to believe. Call on Me and I will heal you. I will harvest all the prayers of healing for you.

PRAYER

Thank You, Jesus, for being the ultimate bringer of breakthrough, especially for my health. Thank You that You have a plan for my body and that You will give me the right tools to work with on my health journey. Thank You, Holy Spirit, that my body is Your temple and that You will nudge me and speak to me about it as I spend time with You. Help me not give any opportunity to insecurity or obsession over my health or body; help me to see it exactly as You do: beautifully and wonderfully made. I give You permission to show me how to improve my health so I can be at full capacity for You and those I love.

Thank You for bringing breakthrough healing to the small and big areas of my need. Thank You for dying and resurrecting so that by the price You paid, I could be restored to Your plan, even in my body. Heal every place of unbelief inside me that wars against truly accepting the fact that You want to heal me. I recognize that, whether out of never seeing You heal this way in my own life or just out of places of doubt, I need more of Your perspective so I can believe for Your healing power.

I don't want to waste one drop of the price Your blood paid on the cross. Help me to enter fully into my destiny of everything You ordained for my body in this season. Keep me from religious exercises that cause me to strive or live in anxiety while I am waiting for Your healing power and grace. Give me confidence in Your love as I wait.

Help me to have a childlike faith that knows You can suddenly perform a miracle, but also keep me strong if it is a process. Help me to surround myself with good news. Share with me stories of others who have gone through similar trials and have overcome. Surround me with Your reports so I can keep refreshing myself in the midst of suffering.

Thank You that not even death can hold back Your power and Your life. I invite You to heal me. I pray for full restoration for every day I have on Earth. Show me how to take care of my temple, my body, in a way that would cause my life to have every access to the health You intended.

"For I am the Lord who heals you."

Exodus 15:26 NLT

"'I will give you back your health and heal all your wounds,' says the Lord."

Jeremiah 30:17 NLT

"The Lord nurses them when they are sick and restores them to health."

Psalm 41:3 NLT

DECLARATION

God, thank You for my health and for my body. I declare that I am fearfully and wonderfully made. Thank You that You had a beautiful plan from when You first thought of me for my body to work to give me full energy and health.

I declare that I am willing to make powerful choices for my own health in regard to food, water, exercise, and what I spend my time doing with my body. I commit to not overmedicating my body using substances You didn't intend for my benefit. I declare that my body is Your temple and I will protect it as I steward it with great love toward You and what You have given me. I commit to listening to You, Holy Spirit, as You gently nudge me in my health journey!

I declare that anything that doesn't line up with this plan would be healed, removed, canceled, and cursed. I speak to my body to be whole, healed, and healthy.

I also declare that my body is no longer bound to any generational patterns and that I won't inherit the negative anymore from my family line or DNA. My line is straight from Your original design and I will live in health all the days You intended for me!

I declare that my body is healthy and healed of any sickness, disease, injury, or ailment that it has been dealing with, and I receive Your healing now, in the name of Jesus!

"How sweet the name of Jesus sounds in a believer's ear! It soothes his sorrows, heals his wounds, and drives away his fear."

—John Newton

MENTAL AND
EMOTIONAL HEALTH

"A cheerful heart is good medicine, but a crushed spirit dries up the bones."

Proverbs 17:22

"You're blessed when you get your inside world—your mind and heart—put right. Then you can see God in the outside world."

Matthew 5:8 MSG

"We can demolish every deceptive fantasy that opposes God and break through every arrogant attitude that is raised up in defiance of the true knowledge of God. We capture, like prisoners of war, every thought and insist that it bow in obedience to the Anointed One."

2 Corinthians 10:5 TPT

"Then Jesus said, 'Come to me, all of you who are weary and carry heavy burdens, and I will give you rest. Take my yoke upon you. Let me teach you, because I am humble and gentle at heart, and you will find rest for your souls.'"

Matthew 11:28–29 NLT

"Lord, I passionately love you and I'm bonded to you! I want to embrace you, for now you've become my power! You're as real to me as bedrock beneath my feet, like a castle on a cliff, my forever firm fortress, my mountain of hiding, my pathway of escape, my tower of rescue where none can reach me. My secret strength and shield around me, you are salvation's ray of brightness shining on the hillside, always the champion of my cause. All I need to do is to call to you, singing to you, the praiseworthy God. When I do, I'm safe and sound in you."

Psalm 18:1–3 TPT

Your keys for breakthrough also are for your emotional health and well-being. God designed your neurology, emotions, and mental capacity to be more than enough to connect to Him and the calling He has for you. He is giving you keys for breakthrough in every aspect of your mental and emotional health.

BREAKTHROUGH PROPHECY

I made you with a powerful mind and passion that was to be carried out in your emotional strength. These tools for your humanity to relate to Me are two of the ones I fight for as your breaker more than any other. I will give you wisdom, understanding, and perspective so you can have health in your emotions and mind.

Your neurology was made to wire with Mine, to think and process the way I do. I will send My spirit to you to relate what is happening deeply within Me and allow you to experience the stability of My own inner life.

When you face emotional or mental pressure or breakdown, I am your comforter. I never designed your mind to stop working or your emotions to be broken; I created you to thrive. Anxiety, fear, depression, mental illness, neurological problems were never My portion for you. I never made you to be lesser in your intellect or to have learning disabilities. I never intended you to have sociological issues in your emotions, but I made you to experience fullness in all of these areas.

I want to give you a vision of what you were made to look like, what My original shape of you looked like for your life so that anything you are settling for no longer is acceptable. I want to show you how I have the power to rewire your mind and thoughts. I can bring an end to emotional whirlwinds, and I want to bring an end to mental distress and illness. These fight against My plan for you to experience a peace that passes all understanding, a joy unspeakable, a fulfillment that goes beyond normal human experience. I have come to bring you an abundant inner life.

Part of how I want to bless you is to bring My love and strength inwardly so you can see a great manifestation of My plans and purposes outside. I want to change the narrative the world has brought inside of you. I want to heal areas that weren't parented with the grace of My love. I want to give you what is in deficit mode inside of you through My spirit.

I want to break off any limitations you have had, even if you were born with them. I never intended you to be born without My fullness, and I want to restore you physically, psychologically, and spiritually.

PRAYER

God, give me the mind of Christ and bring my natural mind and emotions into the right balances. Touch my inner life with Your presence and help me to navigate the difficult places. If I have settled in any area for less than what You intended, help me to have perspective so I can fight for what You have for me.

I pray for my mind to be rewired and for it to work exactly as You intended it. I ask that You would give me clarity of thought, big-picture thinking, and huge perspective for myself and for others. Help me to not get distracted easily, and help me to have the right kind of focus in my life. Father, help me to live out a connected life.

I pray that my emotions would also be rewired and that I would allow the Holy Spirit to be the leader of my mind, body, and emotions. Give me the conviction to do what is right and best, even when I do not feel it. Help Your spirit within me to have a voice bigger than my emotions and thoughts, confirming to me what is in Your nature and what is in Your Word.

"We all experience times of testing, which is normal for every human being. But God will be faithful to you. He will screen and filter the severity, nature, and timing of every test or trial you face so that you can bear it. And each test is an opportunity to trust him more, for along with every trial God has provided for you a way of escape that will bring you out of it victoriously."

1 Corinthians 10:13 TPT

"For God hath not given us the spirit of fear; but of power, and of love, and of a sound mind."

2 Timothy 1:7 KJV

DECLARATION

God of my breakthrough, You created my mind and emotions to have a full capacity of health and strength.

You created me to be wired for the fullness of joy and contentment in my spiritual journey.

I am not deficient in any way, and anything that doesn't work exactly how You intended has to come into alignment with Your original desire and intention for my life.

I was not created to be deficient, have disabilities, have lower intelligence, have mental disorders, have mental illness, have a chemical imbalance, or to have any neurological or psychological issues. I was created to have everything process the way You intended humans to be: in Your image.

Depression, anxiety, fear, compulsion, addiction, distress are not my permanent story or a lifelong label in my identity because You have made me more than a conqueror through Christ Jesus over anything that would cause me to not be able to pursue the life of John 10:10: fullness of life. You will break through in me and for me and give me the keys through my spiritual pursuit of You along with any natural tools You want to use to help me maintain my breakthrough.

My mind and my emotions are fearfully and wonderfully made and You have a plan to heal me, deliver me, and set me free to love how You have created me. Give me patience for the process in those areas that need to develop and faith for those areas that don't yet exist.

*"The pain passes, but the
beauty remains."*

—Pierre-Auguste Renoir

GRIEF AND LOSS

*"So we are convinced that every detail of
our lives is continually woven together to
fit into God's perfect plan of bringing good
into our lives, for we are his lovers who have
been called to fulfill
his designed purpose."*

Romans 8:28 TPT

*"He always comes alongside us to comfort
us in every suffering so that we can come
alongside those who are in any painful trial.
We can bring them this same comfort that
God has poured out upon us."*

2 Corinthians 1:4 TPT

"And the peace of God which transcends all understanding, will guard your hearts and your minds in Christ Jesus."

Philippians 4:7

"He heals the brokenhearted and bandages their wounds."

Psalm 147:2

"For it is written: 'Burst forth with gladness, O barren woman with no children! Break through with the shouts of joy and jubilee, for you are about to give birth! The one who was once considered desolate and barren now has more children than the one who has a husband!'"

Galatians 4:27 TPT

We are human and will experience grief and loss on this side of eternity, but we are not limited to our human responses or understanding of how to handle these complicated issues. We have the God of breakthrough, who gives us keys to understand and to live in a higher way when we face grief and loss.

BREAKTHROUGH PROPHECY

Part of the nature of God being the breaker relates to waterways. Water goes past its normal banks and floods into areas where it normally would never go; it creates waterways where there were no pathways. God is going to break through in your grief and loss situation for you and where people who don't know God are limited to either breaking or to having a normal human resolve of dealing with the pain of these situations. You are going to have the nature of the breaker working deeply within you. He will take impossible pain away from you. He will absorb the sting of death because He has already paid the price on the cross. He will cause His love to go into places that feel like they can't ever be healed. You won't have to live with the condition that grief is your identity.

Jesus Himself said, "Blessed are those who mourn for they will be comforted." This comfort is real, and when you are mourning loss, like the death of a loved one, He will bring a different comfort that is deeper than what your mind can comprehend.

It will be God's spirit working deeply within your spirit, which affects all other aspects of you. There will be a peace where there should have been a hole. There will be sustenance where there should be pain.

God will take away the abandonment that comes to everyone when someone they love dies. He will create an opportunity for you that will go beyond just filling an empty place or distracting loneliness. He will create inside of you a newness. He will be with you as you process your hurt. He will renew your heart to allow love to grow more. What you thought could never happen again will shock you as He brings new love that grows from the seedbed of the old relationship.

For those who lost people who they know went to heaven, He will comfort you by not allowing you to feel they are on pause or gone but that they are still part of your every day as they pray with Jesus over everyone they left behind. Until Jesus returns, they will be part of your cloud of witnesses, praying that no opportunity of God's love is missed in your life. They will be your divine soccer mom, making sure all of heaven knows how important you are and that you get every opportunity even if it seems unlikely for you.

For those who lost someone for whom they have no assurance over their eternal salvation, God wants you to cast that burden on Him. You don't know the thousands of ways God revealed His love to them while they were on Earth. You don't know if their heart ever responded. You don't know if they were like the thief on the cross who in the last moment went to heaven with Jesus. Let Him carry the burden of their salvation. Let Him give you comfort in your loss and the healthy processing of grief you need.

For those who lost a relationship or failed in an opportunity or business, or even a great loss of resource or position, He will take the sting out of the loss. He will not let any shame or anger stay attached to your heart as you walk through the process of allowing wholeness in your heart and mind. He wants to bring His grace to you. Grace in this means He can re-create opportunity; He can redeem what was lost. It is part of His promise as the One who came to redeem all things. He wants to ground your significance in His love for you that there is always a rebuilding and there is always a legacy.

He is never done and He never leaves anyone behind. He is the Good Shepherd and will leave the ninety-nine so the one can come back into fullness. He will work for you so you can have His full measure of life as you believe again. Open your heart to Him. Let Him heal the pain. Cast your cares upon Him and He will give you everlasting love.

PRAYER

Holy Spirit, I want to walk with You through the suffering of grief and loss. Thank You that You draw near to those who mourn and comfort them with Your comfort that is beyond words. I give You my grief process and I ask You to lead me even through the valley of the shadow of death.

I pray that You would empower my hope when it feels like it has died or was lost with this situation. Give me the resolve to hold onto faith in You, and in Your life in me, so I can wake up with expectation and go to bed with true rest, even in the midst of this situation.

Help build in me the expectation that what You have built in me will continue, no matter what was lost. As I lay down some things that no longer fit, help me to see new things that were tailor-made for my new season. Help me to do the impossible: exchange my expectations and exchange everything that was tied into the old thing (that is now gone) for everything You are planning in my *now*. Let disappointment not direct my present or future thoughts and help me to trust and believe for Your grace for my *today*.

Keep me from people who would misunderstand my grief or loss. Keep false advisors and false compassion away from me.

I pray that people who would pity me would be far from me. Surround me with people who are emotionally and spiritually intuitive to what You are doing in my life.

Help me to be a source of empathy and compassion for others who are experiencing loss or grief. Use my wounds, scars, and resurrection of dreams to be a source of hope for others.

DECLARATION

As I face loss or grief, I am believing You to be the God who breaks through and that breakthrough looks like something. I am believing You for:

- A fresh connection to Your love for me and through me

- Restoration in my heart and spirit

- New dreams to replace ones that had to die

- That nothing I loved was in vain, that You will use all the love that was poured out to be a seedbed for this season I am now in of Your goodness—love always wins

- That You can redeem and restore time

- That You heal the sting of death because You defeated it

- That I don't have to live in loss and grief and it is not my condition, although I commit to process it and not hide from it or bury it

- That You are good in the midst of what I don't understand

- That grieving will pass and the feeling of losing someone or something will heal with Your spirit comforting over time

- That my loss will equal huge gain for the kingdom; that You will pay back what has been stolen and lost

- That You are good even though I feel grief and loss; Your goodness is not challenged but will only be revealed to be more real as You walk with me through this and beyond

"Sometimes God brings times of transition to create transformation."

–Lynn Cowell

"When you are transitioning to a new season in life, the people and the situations that no longer fit you will fall away."

–Mandy Hale

"The path to our destination is not always a straight one. We go down the wrong road, we get lost, we turn back. Maybe it doesn't matter which road we embark on. Maybe what matters is that we embark."

–Barbara Hall

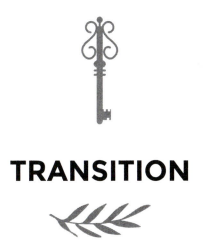

TRANSITION

"And we all, who with unveiled faces contemplate the Lord's glory, are being transformed into his image with ever-increasing glory, which comes from the Lord, who is the Spirit."

2 Corinthians 3:18

"See I am doing a new thing! Now it springs up; do you not perceive it? I am making a way in the wilderness and streams in the wasteland."

Isaiah 43:19

"'For I know the plans I have for you,' declares the Lord, 'Plans to prosper you and not to harm you, plans to give you hope and a future.'"

Jeremiah 29:11

"Don't be pulled in different directions or worried about a thing. Be saturated in prayer throughout each day, offering your faith-filled requests before God with overflowing gratitude. Tell him every detail of your life, then God's wonderful peace that transcends human understanding will make the answers known to you through Jesus Christ. So keep your thoughts continually fixed on all that is authentic and real, honorable and admirable, beautiful and respectful, pure and holy, merciful and kind. And fasten your thoughts on every glorious work of God, praising him always."

Philippians 4:6-8 TPT

One of the keys for breakthrough in your life is the ability to allow change in both your internal and external life. Humans are famous for resisting or even hating change; but as a new creation, God is giving you the ability to live out of your spirit, which longs for transformation even when it means more transition or change is coming. God has a never-ending supply of adaptive energy for you.

BREAKTHROUGH PROPHECY

I have made a promise that I will not just author My plan in your life but will also transform you to become the person you were made to be, inside and out. I will always finish what I start. Transition comes when I invite you into something new that may not have even been something you would have chosen for yourself. My process in your development and to transform the world through you will require a different process than you could accomplish in your own strengths, abilities, or talents. Whereas others who want to have a similar result can just do a normal human process, get an education and pursue a career, I am making you different from the norm. Your life will break open doors that have never been opened before. You will love in ways that are uncommon in what I have called you. Your process will be one that will position you in ways that will cause people to ask, "How did you get here?" and "How did you accomplish this?"

I am refining you through My refining fire, but you will come out on the other end looking at the beauty and authority that you possess through this process and be grateful. You will learn that transition equals promotion.

I am inviting you to lay down what you would choose at times so you can have this different result. I will sometimes ask you to make a choice that is not your first choice, but as you trust Me and sacrifice for Me, as you deny yourself and pick up your cross and follow Me, you will feel like the most connected version of yourself to this life I have given you.

Transition can be painful, but trust Me as I form you. Help others who are going through transitions you see I have initiated. Speak words of comfort to embolden them.

Transition will morph you into something you could have never hoped for or imagined in your wildest dreams.

PRAYER

God, help me to not just endure transition but to consider it an honor, because I know the result it produces. Help me to consider it a privilege when You ask me to make a move, transition, change in my life, even when it creates strain, adaptive energy loss, and natural tension in me. Give me the endurance to persevere. Give me persevering faith.

Thank You that when transition starts, I get to go into a deeper place in my knowing You, from glory to glory. Help me to see You in the midst of all the change. Give me faith for what I will be moving into, as I sometimes have to give up so much while I am moving out of something to attain it.

Thank You that part of You being the God who breaks through is that my transition is for something huge. You have my best interests in Your heart, and You will use this transition to position me, align my life, create deeper perseverance and character in me, and reveal even more of Your love to me. Thank You that understanding You in the midst of transition will help me to love those around me more.

God, as You bring transition in my life, help me to hold onto everything that *can* go with me into the new season. Also, help me to let go of anything that is not for this new time.

Help me to love the change Your transition brings and to not compare it to other transitions You didn't initiate in my life. Help me to be one who is so willing to change that I become one who can help change and reform systems, structures, and lives of those around me with the grace Jesus carried when He was on Earth.

DECLARATION

As You bring transition into my life,
I am believing You for:

- Adaptive energy like I have never had

- Flexibility in my emotions, perspective, and physical and emotional being

- Strength to say yes, even when it is hard

- Perspective on my season and times in life that helps me to keep my sight on the prize of life instead of on the process of change

- Grace in all my relationships as my life changes or as I change; connection to those who are not necessarily changing with me

- A willing heart to change

"God is more interested in your future and relationships than you are."

—Billy Graham

"God can restore most things that were stolen. God will redeem anything that is so broken it cannot be restored. Redemption means recreating as if it never was lost."

—Anonymous

RESTORATION AND REDEMPTION

"A thief has only one thing in mind—he wants to steal, slaughter, and destroy. But I have come to give you everything in abundance, more than you expect—life in its fullness until you overflow!"

John 10:10 TPT

"I, the Lord, sent my army against you. The swarming locusts and the hopping locusts and the destroying locusts and the cutting locusts ate everything you had. But I will pay you back for those years of trouble."

Joel 2:25 ERV

"And God-Enthroned spoke to me and said, 'Consider this! I am making everything to be new and fresh.'"

Revelation 21:5 TPT

"Lord, you are my secret hiding place,
protecting me from these troubles,
surrounding me with songs of gladness!
Your joyous shouts of rescue release
my breakthrough."

Psalm 32:7

"Let my passion for life be restored, tasting
joy in every breakthrough you bring to me.
Hold me close to you with a willing spirit
that obeys whatever you say."

Psalm 51:12 TPT

Jesus came as the breaker to restore all things. He can redeem what can't be directly restored as if it wasn't lost, as if it never needed to be restored in the first place. He is giving you keys for breakthrough to believe for the restoration and redemption of your life, family, community, purpose, resources, and health.

BREAKTHROUGH PROPHECY

I am the Creator who imagined and then created everything and you within My great plan. I never intended you to need restoration or redemption because you are Mine and I love you. I will give you anything you need to be fully connected to Me. I promised this to the first humans who failed in the garden—that One would come from their very relationship and lineage who would restore humanity to Me. I gave them great hope because I could see the greatness inside humanity I created.

I sent My Son to restore all things and to bring redemption from the separation, from the disconnect called sin. I am the One who restored everything and it is My business to keep restoring and redeeming from the smallest details to the universe itself.

When something gets broken, destroyed, or cut off that needs My hand of restoration, lean into Me and watch as what is unraveled comes back together. I will restore your body, your relationships, your finances, your resources, your opportunities, your land, your city, your nation.

Those things that have been so broken that they cannot be restored I express to you My other main promise of the cross redemption: I will take things that can't be restored in this lifetime and re-create them as though they are all new again. When you feel like your sin has defeated your opportunity, watch as My love brings you to a point to restore the time that was lost and re-create your whole destiny as if the potential was never lost. Watch as I redeem time, redeem relationships, redeem purposes. There is no one who is too far out of My redemptive power.

Come to Me. Return to Me. Surrender to Me anything that feels like it can never be put back together and I will restore and redeem. Even when man makes a choice that limits My restorative power, I will always redeem the situation so that your fullness is not limited to another man's decisions. They may divorce you but I will create for you a new plan A. They may win a court case against you but I will bring about a new way to get justice. I am not limited to man's will but am infinitely creative and can bring thousands of solutions to any problem.

Trust Me as I use every situation to show you My love as a Father and to help you in ways that you could never truly help yourself. I have made you to be interdependent with Me. Do not be afraid to press into Me as a Father. Do not be proud. Do not be insecure. It is My joy to restore you and to redeem you. My nature as the One who makes a way for you is also the One who breaks apart any barrier so you can walk in the direction I have for you, no matter what resists you. Trust Me and I will lead you into promises you couldn't have dreamed of or imagined.

PRAYER

Father, I give You every situation that needs Your restoration and redemption. I give You permission to set me up in every area necessary for others to hear Your powerful story of how you redeem my whole life for You. You can have my calendar, relationships, resources, passions, talents, skills, career, ministry. You can have all of me. I pray that You would bring restoration in every area I need breakthrough in. For those relationships and situations that are past restoration, I thank You for bringing me to the point of redemption in which You will re-create full opportunity in all the areas where it didn't work out before, so I can live out the fullness of what You paid a price for on the cross.

I pray that You would restore those around me and bring redemption to those closest to me as well. Start with salvation and then redeem and restore lives. I pray that You would break through in every relationship and situation I have not believed can change or be restored. Renew my perspective so I know how to pray with faith and courage, so I will see in my lifetime Your plan of redemption in its fullness. Help me to not settle for just a little; give me courage to go after all You have for me, even when circumstances have appeared hopeless. I choose to believe in Your restorative nature. You are my redeemer. In Your beautiful name, Jesus, amen!

DECLARATION

I am believing the Breaker to break open restoration and redemption in my life.

I declare that there is no relationship that can't be restored or redeemed. God can either restore or, if it's not a healthy relationship, redeem it and give me the perfect replacement as if it was His original plan A.

I declare that my resources and finances will be restored and rebuilt. Any warfare, bad choices I or others have made against me, market trends or broken investments, any damage I have had inflicted upon me will be restored in my lifetime, not only for me but also it will multiply to my children and their children.

I declare that my time is being redeemed and restored. Any time before I was born again, any time away from God, any time not surrendered to His great purpose, any time that was stolen from wrong relationships or bad opportunities, I declare that God will give me back all time as though it had not been lost. I declare that time will serve my life.

I declare that God will redeem me from the wages of bad decisions and sin. Any area I purposely gave myself over to something consistently that hurt God's heart; any area I didn't protect Him, my spouse, my family, my friends, and my community; and any area of perpetual sin—God is going to save me from reaping all I sowed in my bad choices. He is going to redeem me from having to reap all the consequences of my sin life as I commit to protecting myself, Him, and the relationships I have from this pattern of sin. His goodness is going to redeem my time and save me from myself and the wages of sin as He gives me a brand-new life and makes all things new.

I declare that God is going to redeem and restore my dreams, ambitions, desires, and purpose in life, and allow me to experience the joy of a life well lived, people well-loved through me, and a fulfilled life mission.

"Wealth comes from hard work but not because of hard work. Wealth comes because of God. Everything is His."

–Dave Ramsey

"For every destiny and purpose there is a provision."

–*Keys to Heaven's Economy* (book)

"Most people fail to realize that money is both a test and trust from God."

–Rick Warren

FINANCES

HEAVEN'S ECONOMY

"I will place on his shoulder the key to the house of David; what he opens no one can shut, and what he shuts no one can open."

Isaiah 22:22

"I am convinced that my God will fully satisfy every need you have, for I have seen the abundant riches of glory revealed to me through the Anointed One, Jesus Christ!"

Philippians 4:19

"And God will generously provide all you need. Then you will always have everything you need and plenty left over to share with others."

2 Corinthians 9:8

"I will give you the keys (authority) of the kingdom of heaven; and whatever you bind [forbid, declare to be improper and unlawful] on earth will have [already] been bound in heaven, and whatever you loose [permit, declare lawful] on earth will have [already] been loosed in heaven."

Matthew 16:19 AMP

Here are your keys for breakthrough to resources and finances, which we pray using the term "heaven's economy"—having His keys to His resources to bring breakthrough in your life.

BREAKTHROUGH PROPHECY

You will know God as the God who has broken through in your finances and resources. He is giving you keys to open doors in your company, industry, and business only you have access to. God has designed you to carry authority and to see what He is doing, what He is promoting, and what He wants to release.

He is removing false systems of operation that are man's way, and you are His child, who will reveal His ways. He will shut doors to your industry or business sphere that are old and rusty, immoral, or letting the unrighteous prosper. You have the keys to pray these doors closed, not just open up His doors. He will lead you to pray for the shutting up of where the enemy has tried to use prosperity for his own means.

His spirit is coming on you to give you insight, wisdom, and clarity. You will look at closed doors and immovable problems, but because of the keys you hold, they will open and move for you. People will notice this movement; they will notice this authority. This will draw many to want to be around you, to work with you, to purchase or use your services.

You have keys to doors right now, and as you learn your authority and as He places you within your calling, you will open doors you could have never opened without accessing your relationship with Him. This will cause people around you to wonder how you got to where you are; they will marvel at what God has done for you and they will know you couldn't have accomplished it without Him.

PRAYER

God, I ask You to give me Your keys to the kingdom Jesus promised the disciples. I want to open new doors in my family, life, and industry that have never been opened before or that are not open to me right now. I pray that You would give me the keys to heaven's economy and to resources that will bring about everything I need to fulfill my calling and destiny. I pray that my family and I would access the full provision You have ready for the calling and purposes You have created for us.

I pray that You would use me to also shut doors to sin and to the enemy in my spheres of influence. I also pray You would use my life to shut the door to any activity by the enemy in the sphere I am called to.

As I use the authority You have given me to open up Your doors and release Your economy, I pray that I will have opportunities I could not have produced without You. I pray that my life will not be limited to what I could build with my own best efforts, and that because of my relationship with You, I will receive kingdom opportunities that only come out of my partnership with You.

Jesus, will You help me to live in the economy and provision You paid for on the cross and provided through the power of Your resurrection? Will You help me to be recession proof with my finances and with what I am building? I surrender everything regarding my resources and finances, and I ask You to speak to me about it all so I can succeed in bringing Your dream into this world. Amen.

$

DECLARATION

I declare that God has given me His kingdom keys to finance and resource.

I declare that I am not limited to the natural economy but I am participating with heaven's economy where there are more than enough opportunities, finances, resources, relationships, ideas, and creativity.

I recognize that God has already broken through in the area of my resources and finances, that He has promised me through John 10:10 resources to live the fullness of His life, and that these resources are spiritual, relational, but also natural.

I am committed to partnering with God as the source of all of my opportunities, provision, resources, businesses, relational capital, investments, real estate, and anything He provides for me.

I declare breakthrough of resources and heaven's economy over my life and family, my occupation and workplace, my industry, my street, my neighborhood, and my city. I pray that God would provide everything needed to bring about His full plan.

I ask for ideas, creativity, favor, and opportunities to create heaven's economy on Earth. I pray that God would unlock in me a sense of ownership over His vision for this world and that as I partner with Him, breakthrough will happen in my vision for resources.

I declare that everything I need to see my destiny in Him fulfilled has already been provided by the finished work of the cross, and I declare that it is unlocked to me now in the name of Jesus! Amen!

$

"God will not give you an instruction, assignment, vision or dream without giving you directions, strategies and resources to bring them to pass! Expect breakthroughs, surprises, uncommon favor, promotions & miracles to happen all year long!"

—Dr. Cindy Trimm

"Whatever makes men good Christians makes them good at business."

—Anonymous

BUSINESS AND CAREER

*"The Lord God took the man and put him in
the Garden of Eden to work it
and take care of it."*

Genesis 2:15

*"They were all trying to frighten us,
thinking, 'Their hands will get too weak for
the work, and it will not be completed.' But I
prayed, 'Now strengthen my hands.'"*

Nehemiah 6:9

*"Whatever you do, work at it with all your
heart, as working for the Lord,
not for human masters."*

Colossians 3:23

BREAKTHROUGH PROPHECY

Sometimes it's hard to remember that God prioritizes labor for humanity. He gave it to Adam and Eve as a gift so they would have roles like toiling, reaping and sowing, nurturing, creating community, building family. Oftentimes the areas of business and career are looked at as a means to an end where we want the fruit of our labor but we just do a job when it comes to the labor itself. God wants to give you an assignment over where you work and how you work. He is going to cause your career, job, business, and industry to be places that create His kingdom agenda for you and through you. You won't just live for the finances and significance the role of work creates; you will have a fresh commissioning over the job itself that will bring you great connection to why God created you.

The God who breaks through is bringing breakthrough for business owners and entrepreneurs. He is giving you new ideas, fresh content, connections you would have never made without Him, seed money, angel investors, and resources to do what He has initiated within you. He wants to take you past what you can hope for or imagine in your business, start-up, or job.

God also wants to create synergy and momentum in your relationships. Your career is part of how you get to express the fruit of His love and the power of His character, nature, and gifts. He wants to give you authority where you work. He wants to bring economic justice, strategy, and inspiration through you to your workplace.

In the book of Revelation, the one called the antichrist is seen in the marketplace because that is the strategy of the prince of the air, the devil. He wants to bind up finances, break down significant roles, keep injustice at work in world markets, in politics, in education. He wants to delay ingenuity and put fear in corporations to change or to be innovative. He wants to bring a bad political orphan spirit into the mix so that humanity can't see the goodness of God there. To be anti Christ is to be anti Christ's agenda, and this is so clearly seen in areas of industry and career. God—who King David called *Baal Perazim*, the God who breaks through barriers and comes in like a flood—knows how to break down the enemy's strategies. God wants to use you to be a breaker to the agenda of the enemy and to bring His culture to the kingdoms of this world. God created every right industry, He inspires every career field that can be redemptive, and He wants to give you courage to break through as He breaks in.

God knows the battleground of work, labor, and career. He is going to bring about epic fruit in your life and career as you pursue Him. You will get rare opportunities, promotions that weren't available before you took your role, contracts you had no access to, favor with individuals who are beyond your socioeconomic status. God is choosing you to be His representative and He is empowering you with favor and opportunity.

You will use this favor not to get a better deal or to just bypass the process but to be a favor generator for others.

God wants to create through you a new reputation for Christians working in government, business, education, entertainment, and all industries and fields. Through you He will break off the negative reputation of religious people; you will rebrand what people think about Christians in career fields. People will turn to you for counsel, like Nebuchadnezzar with Daniel. Leaders will look to your governance as Pharaoh did with Joseph.

God is equipping you to carry His divine strength and energy and you will gain such a love for the people who are working in the career path to which you feel freshly assigned. His love will fill you and you will be able to be a friend, advocate, and counselor to people in your workplace. He is going to empower you in ways that don't make sense in the natural but that speak of His love and reality to you and the world around you.

PRAYER

God, I give You my career. I ask to be freshly assigned to my workplace and the staff and team there, and to the industry, city, and nation(s) I work in. I pray that my services or role would be a labor of true love to those around me because of the love You fill me with.

I know that when there is a battle or office politics in the way of my career path, You will not leave me to my own wisdom or resolution but will bring about justice for me, over and over. I pray that You would be at the head of every battle and that You would keep my name out of the mouth of the enemy. Instead, keep it in the mouths of everyone I am called to love.

I pray for open doors only You can open as the Breaker. I ask You for the unusual favor You promised would follow those who surrender their lives to You.

I don't just invite You to be a partner in my career; I also ask for You to be Lord of my career. Lead me in the way You want me to go, and father me in ways no natural mentors would even take the time to. Teach me how to listen and be instructed by Your spirit so that my career isn't just something I do because I have passion for it, but because it's where I begin to truly fulfill the calling You created me for.

Help me to love my work but to not put it in front of my own self-care, in front of my family, or in front of my relationships. I give You my life because You are the great balancer, and I ask that You would show me how to live out of Your perfect boundaries and balance for me.

God, I ask that You would use my time in my career to produce great fruit that would show people that always living a life for You would have a different result compared to the results from someone who is producing by their own abilities and talents. Show up and show off big through my life, God. Help me to not have the wrong kind of pride in my accomplishments. I commit to worshiping You and giving You praise for all You are doing in me and through me. Amen.

DECLARATION

I am believing my God of breakthrough for the best opportunities available to my career. I am believing for:

- Favor for my city and government with CEOs, government leaders, and kings; favor with the IRS or the equivalent; favor with my local city for partnerships and the permits I will need for my business and projects

- Manufacturing firms that produce goods for the nations and provide new jobs for our people

- Technology to establish new markets, energy sources, and efficient solutions to grow as a population

- Laws and courts that measure with the justice and the freedom of our land's Constitution

- Civil servants who encourage entrepreneurs

- A media known for wisdom and truth

- Natural resources released, harvested, sold, and reproduced

- Education, books, and universities that develop mind molders who influence the influential

- Capital to build small businesses that provide services, arts, and culture that attract both the young and the old

- A medical community known for integrity and excellence

- Repentance from poverty, small thinking, and envy

- Courage to recognize opportunities and make wealth

- Entertainment that brings healthy culture to our city, nation, and world; creativity to produce the arts and entertainment that would be celebrated and awarded by culture as it brings the gospel of love through my life

- Abundance to bless the world and the prudence to save and invest

- Revelation to pass on wealth to our children's children

So I declare that when the righteous prosper, the earth rejoices!

(*Part of this declaration is an offering message that is read regularly at Bethel Church in Redding, California, at their services. I have always loved its transformative nature, so I included it to honor them in this book.)

"Breakthrough in ministry cannot be measured by outward success alone, but by the presence of God bringing love to create tangible transformation to those who are your mission."

—Anonymous

✝

CHURCH AND MINISTRY

*"Come and be his 'living stones' who
are continually being assembled into a
sanctuary for God. For now you serve as
holy priests, offering up spiritual sacrifices
that he readily accepts through
Jesus Christ."*

1 Peter 2:5 TPT

*"Then I replied to them, 'The God of heaven
will make us prosper, and we his servants
will arise and build.'"*

Nehemiah 2:20 ESV

*"I hear the Lord saying, 'I will stay close
to you instructing and guiding you along
the pathway for your life. I will advise you
along the way and lead you forth with my
eyes as your guide.'"*

Psalm 32:8 TPT

BREAKTHROUGH PROPHECY

God is preparing the church for the greatest harvest of all times. This harvest is souls. It is maturing to those who already know Him. It is transformation of culture. It is creativity in everything we do. The first time the Holy Spirit filled someone was in Exodus: Bazaleel was filled by the Holy Spirit with creative power to artistically make everything that was needed to bring about connection to God through worship and the temple. God is again filling churches, ministries, and movements with His creative power to bring about everything needed to build a container in our generation that He wants to fill with His love.

We are about to go through another reformation and the God who breaks through is going to break off all kinds of religious mindsets and traditions that no longer bring relational connection to Jesus. He is breaking off small-mindedness and patterns that have us stuck in old ways that are now irrelevant. He is bringing a breakthrough into new ways of thinking, doing, and loving. Just as we have been in the most amazing technological advancement in history, so too we are in the most wondrous kingdom advancement where God is bringing about new tools to bring His same ancient love message to each person living on Earth.

God is giving creative power that will sometimes manifest in healing miracles and sometimes in wisdom for governments, in scripts for movies, or in ministries to unreached peoples.

He is growing new structure through you with new strategy to do church and ministry in ways that have not been done before. You will look for models and God will say, "Become a model." Some ministries and churches that have been around for generations are coming into their promised-land time, no longer just living off the legacy from the glory days; new days are coming with new leadership, strategies and partnerships that will bring about greater moves than you have ever experienced. Forget the former days. Behold! God is doing a new thing you have never seen before.

God is giving us strategies to raise up spiritual sons and daughters and He is changing traditional leadership roles into mentoring fathering roles. Where other generations didn't know how to pass a baton, God is building legacy through movements and churches now, and many strategies will come on how to grow these generationally.

God is resurrecting churches and ministries that have been dying in the wilderness. He is going to set your eyes on the future of what He is about to do instead of the past of what He used to do. He is bringing sons from among you to be your leaders and prophets to bring you into the new place to which He is calling you (see Deuteronomy 18:18).

There will be a homecoming into churches of all the Christians who have been hurt or have not found a place of family within structured ministry. God is going to call masses of people who have been disenfranchised by current ministry or past church experiences back home. The harvest isn't just the souls that are lost; it is a harvest of harvesters who are going to come with deep maturity and walk with a limp of dependency on love because they have wrestled deeply with disappointment and love won!

There will be fresh grace and an outpouring of outward focus on ministries and churches. God will bring the excellence up to a whole other level but not by applying corporate structures. He is going to provide kingdom structures that are even greater containers of community impact and transformation.

Get refreshed! Get renewed! Because God is coming to grow His church.

PRAYER

God, thank You that You love the church and look at it as Your counterpart on Earth. I ask that You would empower our pastors, ministry leaders, and other types of leaders to lay a foundation Your whole kingdom assignment for us can rest on. I ask for revelation that we would see even more clearly the people we are assigned to, the strategy of missions, the connections in our community, and the lands to which we are called. Give me and those who are serving in our churches or ministries Your passion—the passion Paul had—so we will be pregnant with so much of Your love that You, Christ, would be formed in the believers around us.

I pray that You would protect us from infighting, politics, and disunity. Just as You prayed, Jesus, that we would be one, we ask that You would use everything in our lives to make us one. You are the maker of relationships and relational skills. We pray that our churches and ministries would be amazing stewards of relationships that model conflict resolution, healthy boundaries, loyal covenants, nurtured families, godly marriages, and true friendships.

God, give me a transformational mindset so I can believe for lives to be changed and regions, industries, and people groups to be transformed. Help me to see Your original plan for all those to whom I am called to minister. Help me to stand in the gap between where they are now and who You are calling them to be. Help me to take on my mission with love and trust, knowing that it is not my job to fix, change, and save but Yours. Help me to take on the right responsibilities of love so that I let You be the Messiah rather than take on my own Messiah complex. Help there to be no "us" and "them" in my heart between those inside my ministry/church and those outside. I pray that I would feel love, honor, and affection for both those within and those without, even those of other belief systems and contradictory lifestyles to my own.

God of breakthrough, I ask that You would bring breakthrough to my local church, to the movement I am involved in, and to every ministry I or my family are involved in. I give You my expectations for what it has to look like and ask that You would build in me faith for the transformation of organized religion in my generation.

DECLARATION

I declare that through Your love I am going to fulfill my ministry assignment on Earth. I declare that You have called me to love people as my destiny and have given me a calling of ministry to reach them and to have impact that will change lives.

I declare breakthrough strategies for love to invade our mission.

I declare breakthrough power to come against the work of the enemy in our region by filling it with Your purpose and will.

I declare breakthrough success in areas that have been confused and compromised in our community or mission focus.

I declare breakthrough resources so we can do everything You have called us to.

I declare breakthrough favor so we can reach everyone we are called to with Your great love.

I declare breakthrough ingenuity to do things that have never been done before through my assignment.

I declare breakthrough in the ability to reproduce people, spiritual impact, and transformation!

I declare that You won't just add to our ministry/church/calling but that You will multiply it!

"One of the most important things to remember as we face our everyday battles is that standing and resisting the devil doesn't mean being weird. We don't have to act spiritually creepy. God isn't asking us to stir up all kinds of crazy forces or to go after realms we have no business going after. If you run into spiritual resistance in some area of your life, simply take authority and move on (James 4:7). The enemy loves chaos, fear-driven prayers, and an over-spiritualized atmosphere because he loves for us to waste our time focusing on him. Don't give in to that."

—Havilah Cunnington

SPIRITUAL WARFARE

"Rescue me quickly when I cry out to you. At the sound of my prayer may your ear be turned to me. Be my strong shelter and hiding place on high. Pull me into victory and breakthrough."

Psalm 31:2 TPT

"For our struggle is not against flesh and blood, but against the rulers, against the authorities, against the powers of this dark world and against the spiritual forces of evil in the heavenly realms."

Ephesians 6:12

"So then, surrender to God. Stand up to the devil and resist him and he will turn and run away from you."

James 4:7 TPT

"But thanks be to God, who gives us the victory through our Lord Jesus Christ."

1 Corinthians 15:57

"Then he continued, 'Do not be afraid, Daniel. Since the first day that you set your mind to gain understanding and to humble yourself before your God, your words were heard, and I have come in response to them. But the prince of the Persian kingdom resisted me twenty-one days. Then Michael, one of the chief princes, came to help me, because I was detained there with the king of Persia.'"

Daniel 10:12

This is a big one. We all need God as a breaker for us at one point in life. As we follow our passion and calling to fulfill our destiny, the Bible models for us that the enemy who is out to destroy us was defeated by the finished work of the cross. We still wrestle but the war is won. Here are your keys for receiving God's breakthrough in your life in the battles as you continually see He has won the war.

BREAKTHROUGH PROPHECY

You are My greatest love, My greatest asset, My treasure among treasures. Anything that wars against you is My highest priority. I am the God of angel armies and I will commission all of heaven on your behalf. Whether the war is with sickness, finances, relationships, government, or anything else, I am coming, I will come, and I will work anything that has hurt you for your good [see Romans 8:17]. That means that what the enemy meant for evil against you will actually serve you. When people slander you, I will use it to build your reputation in others' hearts. I will turn the seed of gossip into a favorable connection or multiply your reputation for every person the enemy tries to destroy it with. When people unjustly sue you, I will bring about blessings and connection from other sources while fighting for a justice that is even greater than your victory in courts. When your government persecutes you, I will walk with you and fight for you as you follow Me. I will fight for your name, reputation, and honor.

I will tenderly restore what the enemy is trying to kill, steal, or destroy. I have come to bring you the purest abundant life you can have. I want you to experience My grace, blessing, and favor on this side of eternity; it is yours now.

Just like Daniel, from the first time you humbled your heart before Me, I sent help. Even if it feels delayed, I am fighting your battle and I have never lost a fight.

To you the enemy is a dragon roaring, but to Me he is a worm. I am God and I will give you a roar louder than the enemy. I will cause the enemy to tremble for choosing to pick a fight with you. I will get justice that will go beyond your lifetime.

PRAYER

God, train me how to fight the battle in front of me. Be my breakthrough and fight through me and for me. Let my fight not be against people but against the injustice of wrongly positioned powers and spiritual principalities. Help me to fight by bringing Your kingdom of love and power, not by shouting at enemies I don't need to engage with. Teach me to use the words You used over demonic spirits: "The Lord rebuke you, Satan." God who breaks through, rebuke my enemies. Cause the things the enemy meant for evil to serve me.

"In all these things, we are more than conquerors through Him who loved us."

Romans 8:37

"Everyone look! Come and see the breathtaking wonders of our God. For he brings both ruin and revival. He's the one who makes conflicts end throughout the earth, breaking and burning every weapon of war."

Psalm 46:8–9 TPT

DECLARATION

Psalm 91 is one of our most powerful passages of Scripture to stand on in times of warfare. Using the Bible as a direct declaration tool is essential so you can learn to stand firm on the truths that not only define your belief system but that also become the foundation for the Spirit to become the director of your thoughts, emotions, and world. Read Psalm 91:1-16 as a declaration over yourself. Let it become a mantra in seasons of attack:

> 1: When you sit enthroned under the shadow of Shaddai, you are hidden in the strength of God Most High.

> 2: He's the hope that holds me and the stronghold to shelter me, the only God for me, and my great confidence.

> 3: He will rescue you from every hidden trap of the enemy, and he will protect you from false accusation and any deadly curse.

> 4: His massive arms are wrapped around you, protecting you. You can

run under his covering of majesty and hide. His arms of faithfulness are a shield keeping you from harm.

5: You will never worry about an attack of demonic forces at night nor have to fear a spirit of darkness coming against you.

6: Don't fear a thing! Whether by night or by day, demonic danger will not trouble you, nor will the powers of evil launched against you.

7: Even in a time of disaster, with thousands and thousands being killed, you will remain unscathed and unharmed.

8: You will be a spectator as the wicked perish in judgment, for they will be paid back for what they have done!

9–10: When we live our lives within the shadow of God Most High, our secret hiding place, we will always be shielded from harm. How then could evil prevail against us or disease infect us?

11: God sends angels with special orders to protect you wherever you go, defending you from all harm.

12: If you walk into a trap, they'll be there for you and keep you from stumbling.

13: You'll even walk unharmed among the fiercest powers of darkness, trampling every one of them beneath your feet!

14: For here is what the Lord has spoken to me: "Because you have delighted in me as my great lover, I will greatly protect you. I will set you in a high place, safe and secure before my face.

15: "I will answer your cry for help every time you pray, and you will find and feel my presence even in your time of pressure and trouble. I will be your glorious hero and give you a feast.

16: "You will be satisfied with a full life and with all that I do for you. For you will enjoy the fullness of my salvation!"

"As a Christian when your trial is getting hotter you are getting closer to your breakthrough. Keep pressing in!"

—Heidi Baker

"You have a breaker anointing. You are one who is going to break through the gates of the enemy and God will break in through you into industries, nations, and places that God's love is rare."

—Jill Austin

"The gates of your greatest breakthrough are formed from your greatest struggles."

—Bill Johnson

TO BECOME A BREAKER IN EVERY AREA

"The 'One Who Breaks Through Walls' will push through and walk to the front of his people. They will break through the gates and leave that city. They will leave with their king marching before them—with the Lord at the front of his people."

Micah 2:13 ESV

"Then David went to Baal Perazim and defeated the Philistines in that place. He said, 'The Lord broke through my enemies like water breaking through a dam.' That is why David named that place 'Baal Perazim.'"

2 Samuel 5:20

"The Lord will fight as he did at Mount Perazim and in the valley of Gibeon, in order to do what he intends to do—strange as his actions may seem. He will complete his work, his mysterious work."

Isaiah 28:21 GNB

BREAKTHROUGH PROPHECY

I want to release a breaker anointing that will break open this world with My kingdom through you. I will break open places that feel immovable right now. There is an invasion from heaven that will break open territory in your lives and families for My purpose.

As your breaker, I am going to break open pathways you could never have seen open that will show that My favor and love are covering you.

As your breaker, I will break through the enemy's line and take you into the land I promised. You can either see the promised land filled with giants because of your weakness and you will never possess it, or you can see that it is a land of milk and honey and that the giants are little compared to what I am capable of. Part of being a breaker is actually having the perspective to see who I am and what I want on Earth right now. It is a prophetic edge that sees what is available through Me that cannot be attained without Me.

You are going to be seen as one who forges new paths, blazes new trails, makes a way where there previously was no way. It won't just be a pioneering spirit; it will be proof that I didn't just come to deliver this world from the enemy and his kingdom but that I came to deliver My people back into the fullness of My promise.

I have put a breaker anointing to bring ingenuity in and through you—inventiveness, reformational thinking, creativity. You will restore and redeem what has been lost but you will also bring about what I intended that no man has yet seen. The kingdoms of this world constantly recycle the fruit of what I brought in past moves; but you serve the kingdom of the God of breakthrough and I will bring My newness of life and will create in ways that will astound people with sign upon sign and wonder upon wonder.

Come and know Me as I revealed Myself to David in the valley of the giants. Come and see Me as I revealed Myself to Solomon when he invited My glory to fill everything he built for Me, when he asked Me to fill the very nation and temple. Let Me fill you as My temple and give you wisdom that will confound the wise and power that will feel like it's from another age and time.

Let My love be the greatest breaker, My love that finds a way where there was no way before. Your life will bring so much salvation, so much fruit, and so much purpose if you let Me bring My presence on your life to break open the kingdom I have called you to walk in on Earth as it is in heaven.

PRAYER

God, You made me in Your image, and part of Your image is that of the Lord who breaks through. I ask that You would fill me with Your nature and give me a breaker anointing like the one Micah talked about. Help me to be the breakthrough for my family, my friends, my industry, my ministry, my city, my country, and this world. Help me to have greater connection and intimacy with You so Your creative mind fills me; and through this deep connection, help me to break open people, systems, and even nations that are stuck right now and to never get stuck.

God, I know the world is crying out for solutions to problems, justice for injustice, and life in place of death. I pray that You would use my life to bring about Your love and to break open light where there is a deep darkness covering the earth. Thank You that Your glory illuminates Your love and that I get to be a part of bringing salvation to Earth, engaging culture, and seeing nations transformed.

Help fill me with Your perspective that the promised land isn't just a land of giants and that You are big enough to clear out all the enemies, and that I get to possess it with You and for You. Help me to have a victorious attitude when I look at my life and the world around me. Create in me the positive attitude of a breaker so when people interact with me, they can feel that through You, all things are possible. Amen.

DECLARATION

I am a breaker. I am called to break open new paths with new ideas.

I am called to make a way where there seems to be no way.

I am called to break through the lines of enemies and win the victory for the justice of heaven.

I am called to invent, create, bring ingenuity, and change.

I am called to be the breakthrough in my love for those I am in relationship with, helping them become the best versions of themselves.

I am not called to see what the enemy is doing and what man is doing wrong, but I am called to have a breakthrough perspective by seeing what God is doing and what He wants.

I am called to break through in territories for which only faith will give me authority. I am called to be a pioneer and leader.

I am called to build upon what God has done through the legacy of generations of Christians, not paying the price that has already been paid but taking the price and cashing it in for new tools, reformed thinking, new moves of God's spirit, new revival, and transformation.

Because I am a breaker, I will never be stuck, never hit a roadblock I can't break through with God's love and power, never take no for an answer when I know God is saying *yes*! I will never back down from a fight God has already given me the victory for, never stay in a wilderness when there are mountains to shout from, and never settle for plan B because plan A looks impossible.

As a breaker, I will see God move in ways no generation has ever seen before, and I will see souls come into the kingdom and people be transformed.

I am a breaker and I serve the God whose love has broken through.

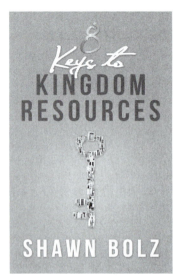

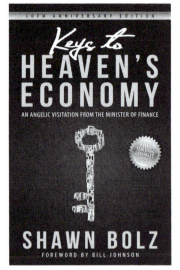

8 KEYS TO KINGDOM RESOURCES

Shawn Bolz presents 8 amazing keys to accessing kingdom resources. God wants you to steward great resources more then you want to.

It is He Who gives you power to get wealth, that He may establish His covenant which He swore to your fathers, as it is this day.
• Deuteronomy 8:18 •

1. Giving and generosity
2. Finance, resources, and time
3. Favor, relationships, and influence
4. Hard word
5. Creativity
6. Education
7. Risk and faith
8. Intimacy with God

KEYS TO HEAVEN'S ECONOMY

So begins the unfolding of Shawn Bolz's visitations from God's heavenly messenger, His minister of Finance.

Heavenly Resources have only one purpose–that Jesus Christ would receive his full reward and inheritance in our age. Just as God held nothing back from Solomon, who longed to build a tabernacle for God on earth, God will hold nothing back from a generation of people who long to bring Jesus everything that belongs to Him!

God is about to release finances and resources to reshape the Body of Chris on the earth. God is looking for those who desire an open-door experience with the One who is the Master of all keys, Jesus

Keys to
HEAVEN'S
ECONOMY
E-COURSE

DISCOVER THE KEYS
TO UNLOCKING
YOUR DESTINY

WWW.BOLZMINISTRIES.COM

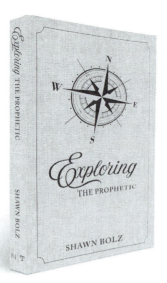

EXPLORING THE PROPHETIC 90 DAY DEVOTIONA

Learn how to tap into the knowledge of God, hear his voice clearl
and share his words. Cultivate your knowledge of God's heart and min
with these daily intentional steps, deep questions only God can answe
thought-compelling points, and Scripture and questions for personal re
flection. Even if the last three months of your life haven't grown your spi
itual life much, you can make the next three incredible with the help c
this 90-day devotional. Your growth will not only bless those around yo
you will also find your own relationship with God transforming into some
thing even more heartfelt and personal than it already is. Read, stud
change, and get ready to impact the world.

www.bolzministries.com

PROPHETIC ECOURSE 101
WITH SHAWN BOLZ

AN IN-DEPTH STUDY OF THE PROPHETIC

EXPLORING THE
PROPHETI
BE CURIOUS WITH SHAWN BOLZ
WILL FOR
APOSTLE GUILLERM
JAMES KRAME
MICHAEL MCINTYR
BILL JOHNSO
KAREN GIBSO
ANTONY ARIS-OSUL
DOYIN LAYAD
PHIL SMIT
BRIAN HEAD WELC
TOMMY GREE
EDWINA FINDLE
SARA BOWLIN
SEAN FEUC
AMY WAR
MATT TOMME
BOB HASSO
CINDY MCG
BO LZ
PODCAST

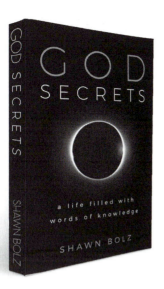

G O D
S E C R E T S
a life filled with
words of knowledge

DID YOU KNOW YOU CAN GROW IN WORDS OF KNOWLEDGE?

Paul encourages believers in 1 Corinthian 14:1, to follow after love and to eagerly desire the gifts of the Spirit, especially prophecy. He would never tell us to pursue something or give us hope for certain gifts if we couldn't engage them! Words of Knowledge is one of the revelatory gifts that we can grow and strengthen just like any other spiritual gift. God loves to tell us specific information about people that we wouldn't naturally know on our own! God has been known to reveal birthdates, anniversaries, family nicknames, pet names, and even bank account numbers at times! The sharing of these personal details help to develop trust and strong connection to the Lord. It produces faith to believe that God deeply loves them and that He truly does have plans to prosper them and give them a hope for their future!

---

www.bolzministries.com

TRANSLATING GOD

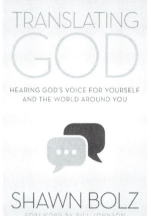

Through a thought-provoking prophetic ministry philosophy and Shawn's glorious successes and very real failures, you will be inspired and equipped to: learn how to hear God for yourself and others, grow through simple focused steps, take great risks, stay accountable, love people well, grow in intimacy with the Lord.

As an internationally known prophetic voice who has ministered to thousands from royalty to those on the streets Shawn shares everything he has learned about the prophetic in a way that is totally unique and refreshing. Shawn aims for the higher goal of loving people relationally, not just pursuing the gift or information, and he activates you to do the same.

Start to reshape the world around you with God's love today.

TRANSLATING GOD WORKBOOK

Be activated by Shawn's inspirational stories and use the activations, questions, and forms he includes in this life-altering workbook to chart your progress. Either individually or in a group, learn how to:

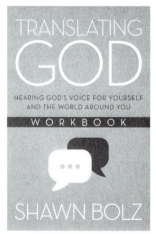

- Develope your relationship with God and others.
- Receive and understand revelation.
- Intentionally develop and nurture your prophetic ability.
- Become the fullness of God's expression of love through his revelation and voice.

www.BolzMinistries.com

MODERN PROPHETS

A TOOLKIT FOR EVERYONE ON HEARING GOD'S VOICE

HEOLOGICAL AND EXPERIENTIAL REFORMATION ON PROPHECY!

phecy is not just about hearing God's voice, but administering God's will very area of life. Much of the prophetic today is elusive and unapproache. Practical tools of healthy theology are changing everything.

dreams and desires of God for every person are made available through phecy. Business plans are perfected, kidnapped victims are discovered, vernment officials elected by means of this gift.

benefits are truly endless. It's time we become Modern Prophets. Learn v to administrate the gift, ministry, and office of Prophecy. Go on a journey ncorporating the prophetic into your life.

dern Prophets makes the prophetic useful, practical, and real in every ere of society!

GROWING UP WITH GOD

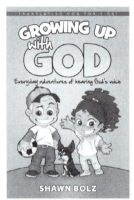

Chapter Book

JOIN LUCAS AND MARIA AND FRIENDS
ON THEIR EVERYDAY ADVENTURES IN
FRIENDSHIP WITH GOD!

Lucas knows God talks to him, but he would have never imagined that he would hear such a specific thing about his year . . . and could Maria really have heard God about her destiny? They both have to wonder if God speaks to kids this way. Over the months that follow, God begins to connect them to other kids that grow into friends. Who could have guessed that by the end of the year, their lives would be so exciting!

Award-winning illustrator Lamont Hunt illustrates the rich, vibrant God journey of kids you can relate to. By best-selling author Shawn Bolz.

Workbook

An accompaniment for *Growing Up with God*, the children's chapter book, this workbook will encourage your kids to practice hearing God's voice.

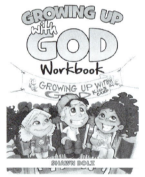

Not only does this workbook teach children how to listen to God, it also gives them the tools they need to support and believe in themselves and each other.

In each section that relates to a chapter in *Growing Up with God*, your children will find:

- A reminder of what was in the chapter
- A true story from a kid their age about how he or she encountered God
- Three important things to know about God's voice
- Bible verses to back up the teaching
- Questions for them to think about and answer
- A prayer
- Illustrations from the book to keep the content focused & exciting

This generation of kids will be the most powerful, prophetic generation yet, and this workbook is a journal and guide will help them fulfill that destiny.